Answers From The

Akashic Records

Volume 3 (of 100)

Down-stepped By Aingeal Rose & Ahonu

Published by Twin Flame Productions LLC

Series Info: 3rd in the Series
Answers From The Akashic Records
Library of Congress cataloging in publication data

O'Grady, Aingeal Rose, 1953 –
O'Grady, Kevin (Ahonu), 1958-
Answers From The Akashic Records Volume 3
Aingeal Rose & Ahonu.

ISBN-10: 1-68323-057-4

ISBN-13: 978-1-68323-057-1

Designed and Edited by: Aingeal Rose & Ahonu
From a session on 19 May 2013.
Artwork: AHONU.com
Published by Akashic Records Press,
an imprint of Twin Flame Productions LLC
Printed in the United States of America

Dedication

Some of the profound statements in this book:

"Our intention is our prayer",
"Prayer donates spiritual energy
to the world",
"Economic collapse can be a cleansing
of the unnecessary",
and "It will take 70% of the people
to actualize a new Earth."

This book is our prayer,
to our cleansing of the unnecessary,
and the actualizing of a new Earth!

Table of Contents

Author's Note

Hello! My name is Ahonu, and along with my wife and Twin Flame Aingeal Rose, we welcome you to **Answers From The Akashic Records**. You are probably here just like all of us, searching, seeking, looking for answers to the deeper questions of life.

We have been through the dis-information, the lies, the deceit, the coercion, the power and control that has kept us enslaved for eons. We have been injected with mercury from vaccines, inhaled chemtrail-filled air, drunk the fluoridated water, been bombarded with electro-magnetic radiation, eaten irradiated and genetically modified food, and listened to the nonsense and lies coming from our politicians, priests and teachers. But we always knew there was truth we were not being told. We knew the old ways didn't work, but believed there were no alternatives. So, we continued to obey, and abide by the old rules, and remained enslaved in our own minds, and carried on working 9-5 every day, paying taxes and growing old.

Our world may be in deep trouble and we know we are in a time of major change. We find that some people can move through these changes easily while others struggle with depression, illness and disorientation. We understand that those reading this may have been experiencing the same thing — we have felt it ourselves, and there seemingly was no solution.

For this reason, Aingeal Rose and I decided to invite people to come to weekly group sessions to inquire into the Akashic Records for the purpose of understanding our world, our spirituality, our Earth changes and more. Aingeal Rose had been accessing the Akashic field for over 25 years doing private consultations for people around the world. You are reading the results.

In these volumes of practical spirituality in a changing world, you will find answers to questions about Consciousness, Twin Flames & Soul Mates, Kundalini, Chakras, Gifted Children, Fairies, Healing, Lightbodies, God, Creation, The Future, Inner Earth, Conception, Saints, Longevity, DNA, Marijuana, Free Energy, Famous Deceased, Stress, Prophecies, Prayer, Joy, Christian Sacraments, Alchemy, Dolphins & Whales, Symbolism in your Everyday Life, What the Trees Have to Say, What the Water, the Oceans, the Sky, and the Land has to say.

You will find answers about the Solar System, Crystals, Earth, Evolution, Technology, Luck, Karma, Planes of Existence After Death, Time, Timelines, Ghosts, Spirits, Multidimensional Selves, Sacred Geometry and more topics asked by people around the world.

The answers to these questions became the basis for Aingeal Rose's first book called *A Time of Change* which is available from http://atimeofchange.info. Her 2nd book, called *The Nature of Reality* can be ordered from http://thenatureofreality.info.

For more information about us and our work, go to: https://worldofempowerment.com. There you will find testimonials, podcasts, healing services, home study courses, private consultations, books, audio books, downloads and more.

This is the time for accelerated advancement and we can all *'catch the wave'*. It is our intention that these volumes will help you shift and adjust to the demands of this time period because this time period is offering the potential for great illumination, joy and blessings. We offer you this information from Source via the Akashic Records and hope you will experience peace, understanding, illumination and personal betterment from what is contained herein.

Aingeal Rose & Ahonu
Central Oregon
December 2016

Introduction

About The Akashic Records

The Akashic Records is a *'place'* in spirit, a vast library, where the events of creation and everything in it is recorded. Everyone has access to the Akashic Records where all these answers are held if they are able to tune into them. The Records are a field of knowledge about creation and the movement of our lives. This is why we felt it was the perfect place to look for the answers to humanity's questions.

So, if you have been confused, unsure, uncertain, or just plain curious about life and the Earth — you will find many answers here in these volumes. You will be surprised at the amount of profound content in the form of video, audio and transcripts that we have collected from our many sessions into the

Akashic Records and in our conversations with Source. Indeed, in this series of print, ebook, and audio books alone, we have 100 completed sessions in the Akashic library to date, and each month we add more!

Each session is between 1-1½ hours, making the collection at the moment over 120 hours of deep, loving, life-changing content! Each session contains an average of 40 profound statements from the Akashic Records, bringing the total number of statements to over 4,000!

We believe this is one of the largest collections of Akashic Records content in the world, and we are grateful to be able to offer this information to you during this major time of change on Earth.

Remember, that throughout these sessions, Aingeal Rose was not in a trance and neither was she channeling through any spiritual or psychic entity, spirit, angel or ascended master. She simply down-steps this information and knowledge directly from Source. This book contains the transcript of one of those broadcasts. The transcripts are shown in their original Question & Answer format.

If you'd like to learn how to read the Akashic Records, check out our home-study course here: http://akashicrecords.smartmember.com/course-details

Answers From The Akashic Records

Q. What is Source's definition of the Akashic Records?

A. Source's definition is that it is a field of information like streams of color or spheres of light, and not necessarily language.

It is similar to different frequency bands of information which vibrate as different colors or resonate as sounds.

It is part of the collective unconscious where everything that ever was or ever will be, resides.

It is the same as saying that it is the 'all that is'.

Once something is added to it, it IS — in other words — it EXISTS.

Once something exists, it is there in the field and it registers as different colors or frequencies of information.

Q. What's the purpose of the Akashic Records?

A. It's like asking 'what's the purpose of existence' — because they are one and the same. The Akashic Records are records of existence — of everything that exists and existence is for God's pleasure.

Q. Are the Records open all of the time or are some Records closed or sealed?

A. God's information is open to everyone and is free to everyone, all the time. There are no Records that are closed, however, if you are not at a certain level of consciousness, there are Records you could not access or read. Since they are a collection of frequencies, your ability to access the Memory, or the 'all that is' has everything to do with your own state of consciousness.

Q. Are there specific 'rules' to access these Records?

A. There are no rules per se, however it is a vibrational field and accessibility has everything to do with your own state of consciousness. So the 'rules' are, you can't access it unless your state of consciousness is a vibrational match.

Q. Are there specific prayers to access the Records or would an intention suffice?

A. There is more than one prayer that can be said, but more than that, it is about your intention. Anyone with the wrong intentions would not be able to access certain frequencies. The advantage of particular prayers is that they will take you to certain frequencies and your ability to align yourself to those frequencies will determine how able you are to read the Records. Specific prayers do make a difference.

Q. Where are the Records located?

A. Everywhere, throughout all existence.

Q. Are there different locations for different Universes or are they all in the same place?

A. Again, it is about frequency. In one sense you could say that everything exists simultaneously but you would not necessarily have access to every universe if you are not vibrationally compatible with it. Certain Records would not be found in certain alternate universes if you did not have experiences in those places. In other words, since we are talking about resonances, my Records may not be 'located' in another Universe if I, as a soul never went there or imprinted a frequency of myself there. Each person's Records would be contained within the fields where they resonate and have their experiences.

* * *

Q. Can the Records be changed?

A. No, they can only be added to. Let's say science/technology has discovered a way to go back into the past and change an event — the original event is still recorded as it happened. You can't go back and take something out of existence once it has existed. You are really creating a new event in a certain time period, but you are not taking away the old event.

Q. Who are the 'Lords' of the Records?

A. They are Beings whose job it is to 'guard' them — they make sure each person's Records do not get mixed vibrationally with another's. They are not Beings who demand any kind of permission. As mentioned previously, the Records have their own safeguards against those with impure intent.

Q. Is the name 'Lords' an appropriate name for them?

A. Yes — the name 'lord' in this case means 'overseer' or 'guardian'. It does not refer to any kind of adoration or hierarchy.

Q. Do you need to ask these Lords for permission to access these Records?

A. No. It is their job to keep the Records in

order. As mentioned previously, the Records have their own safeguard for entry and access. The permission is asked to gain access of the person being read, and it is they and their own higher aspects that agree to this.

Q. How does that make sense if we're all the same — if, at a spiritual level, we're all One? Why are there Beings to keep us separate if we are meant to be unified?

A. Each individual soul is on its own journey to Self-Realization. You are misunderstanding 'unified' or 'one'. Unity does not mean everyone dissolves into one thing. Unified means 'in harmony with'. It means that you understand that everything is in relationship with everything else — we all affect each other — it's a Unified Field in that way — but it doesn't mean that you don't have individuality. It is like the definition of Love — Love is the field of all that is — it doesn't mean it is one big identity in which you lose yours.

Q. Are there different levels of Records and if so, where are they and what do they pertain to?

A. There are different levels of Records in that there are different Universes and differing frequency ranges in those Universes. You may call it levels if you wish. They pertain to the experiences of those Universes where they are.

* * *

Q. If all time is simultaneous, how does it register something as having 'happened'?

A. Where is the confusion? Once something has happened, it is there. It doesn't have a distinction with time; it is part of the whole, which is timeless. Past, present or future is not separated — it just IS.

Q. Who are the 'Mentors'? Where do they come from and how are they assigned?

A. They are Spiritual Beings who are specific to each person's soul journey or to a soul family. They are assigned at the birth of the soul or soul family and remain with it/them throughout its journey within that galactic family. They come from a collective sphere of light. As the soul ascends to Higher Universes, new Mentors are assigned.

Q. What can we gain from accessing our Akashic Records?

A. Accessing your Records will bring you a deep understanding of who you are and why you are here. You can understand health issues, lessons learned and yet to be learned, karmic imprints, relationships, and know your highest gifts and abilities. You will also gain a greater appreciation for the value of choice and the effect choices have on your soul journey as well as its effect upon others and the whole. Moreover, you will know HOW MUCH YOU MATTER and how much a part of everything you are. You will know you are loved and that life does indeed, make sense and have an order to it.

Q. is it possible to teach anyone to read the Records or do they have to be quite advanced spiritually to down-step Truth?

A. You can teach a prayer to anyone and that prayer can help someone reach a certain frequency level, but, how able that person is to match that frequency or down-step the information has everything to do with their own abilities. The exception to this would be to go into a hypnotic state similar to Edgar Cayce, where the perceptual filters are bypassed and would not be interfering. Keep in mind, however, that with the hypnotic process, the translator could be susceptible to wear and tear on his mind and body if he or she is not naturally attuned to those higher frequencies.

Q. What about predicting the future in the Records?

A. You can see probable futures. Certain events may not be in your timeline. Indeed, you are always at choice and can avoid certain outcomes through awareness of this choice.

* * *

Q. Are certain people better able to access the Records than others, and if so, how does this affect the information coming through?

A. Yes, certain people are able to access the Records better than others, which does affect the translation coming through in the down-stepping process. It has to do with an individual's own filters of consciousness, i.e., their opinions and belief systems can taint the purity of what they can receive.

Q. Can you erase your own Records and is it desirable to do so?

A. Nothing is ever lost but what does go is a certain attachment to an event, time period, experience, person, etc. When we talk about erasing the Records, we are talking about erasing the 'charge' that's attached to them. It is a way of reconciling events. Think of it as psychic energy or cords that you may have to certain aspects of your Records — some might call it 'karma'. It is desirable to go back into your own past and reconcile your own past so that it is recorded as memory, but there are no longer any cords. You don't really erase it out of the 'Book', but you do erase the attachment or anything left undone or not forgiven.

Remember, we were talking about the Records being frequencies — any frequencies that lock parts of you 'in place' or anchor you to a certain event or time period need to be reconciled. That way your 'time stream' is clean — it becomes frequencies of beautiful, harmonious ribbons of colors as opposed to frequencies that would keep you locked in a place or time.

For example, you really wouldn't want a prior lifetime still affecting you today, keeping you from being free. This is what is interesting about reading your own Records or your own 'Book' — you can see where you still have things to resolve. You can also see what you've gained — you can get a good measure of yourself.

Q. Can anybody get into your personal Records without your permission?

A. Yes and no. If they can access your frequency, yes, and no, if their intention is not honorable or if there are lessons personal to you that need self-discovery, they will see a blank wall of energy preventing them from reading. The Records have their own safeguard against person's whose intentions are not honorable in that their frequency will not be high enough to access the Records. Anyone trying to read another's Records without their permission is not acting honorably. In principle, the Records are open books, but not in application. It's a perfect system.

The Session

Aingeal Rose (AR): Welcome to our third Akashic Records book. It was down stepped on Mother's Day, and we all know how important that beautiful Divine Mother energy is. Thank you for being with us. Okay, let's get started. I'm going to go ahead and say the prayer and then we'll be ready.

… Aingeal Rose says the prayer…

Beautiful blue light today, filling the room. It's a beautiful royal blue, which feels just so peaceful and calm. So, let's go ahead with questions.

Question One

Ahonu: Some humans are born with their past life memories intact and they have strong psychic abilities. Some also have horrible early life experiences and a strong darkness like a Jekyll and Hyde personality. Please explain?

AR: Many of these children lived in time periods where the technology was very advanced and they have been part of creating that technology. Some are the people who didn't use this technology in the best way. Part of what's happening is these children are coming back with the same genius and the same psychic abilities, but also with some of their own personal karma to work out from these past lives. They are beings who lived in either advanced civilizations or more recent civilizations where they possibly misused power. They are here to balance this karma and use their genius to progress the planet forward instead of control it.

We have to remember that this time period we're all now in is for the accelerated cleansing of our many lifetimes and the karma attached to them, if any. Some of these children could also have a contract to rehabilitate a fallen being inside their own biology. If a child has this type of contract, it is a very difficult one to have. They would have agreed to this before incarnating. The word *'rehabilitate'* is really important here because sometimes beings fall so far into darkness that it is very difficult for them to resurrect themselves on their own. Another way to say it is that their biology may be so damaged that the potential needed to evolve to higher levels may no longer be there. Sometimes a more advanced being will agree to carry a fallen being within their own biology as a way to help the fallen being rehabilitate itself structurally by merging with the gene coding of the advanced being — in this case, the advanced child.

This expresses itself as a person who appears to have two sides to them. It is not really that, but rather another being is actually living inside the advanced child's biology. This often produces extreme conflicts within the one carrying the fallen being, and you will see what appears to be a light and dark battle expressing itself.

It's a hard contract because there is an inner struggle between the advanced being and the fallen being. Even though each being has agreed to the rehabilitation, the process is not easy.

Question Two

Ahonu: In prior sessions from Source It warns about cloning. Can you talk more about that? What about the cloning of embryo's from stem cells?

AR: Source has told us that cloned beings won't live very long because they don't have an individuated spirit that chooses to come into incarnation. The individuated spirit is what keeps propelling the spirit onward toward greater growth and progress. A cloned being does not carry the same spirit energy and the same soul energy as the original being, therefore it is lacking in the vital life force energy that comes from the original spirit.

As I am looking at a cloned being or animal, I feel incredible compassion for them. Here is this new life form that is really severely lacking the elements that it needs to function as a full being in its own species. Source advises us to give these cloned beings love.

That will start to change their structure. If we were to imagine holding these cloned beings in our arms and giving them love and acknowledging them as a valid life form, it could begin to change its DNA. That's the answer that I'm getting because it doesn't look like we can stop scientists from experimenting with cloning. They consider this a really good experiment.

Cloning organs, however, seems to be beneficial only if it's used for the same person. In other words, if you had a bad liver and scientists knew how to clone your own liver and then put the cloned liver into you, the cloned liver would integrate into you because it is already compatible with you. So in those cases it can be beneficial.

Question Three

Ahonu: Spiritually, what is behind the bad economic downturn in the USA?

AR: Source is saying that part of it is because we are really off-center, we've lost our connection to our spirituality and our inner selves, and we've become too materialistic. This downturn is not a punishment by Source — rather it's an attempt at balance.

If we really take a look at what's going on financially, the spiritual lessons that we could get out of this is to seriously look at our dependence on external things in general and also how much of our own identity we've put into whether we have a good financial life or not. Source's desire for us is to get reconnected to things that have true meaning:

- Intimacy with all life.
- Greater connection to Nature.
- Stopping to smell the roses.
- Taking time to look at what really

matters.

- Understanding how much we really waste.
- Understanding how much we don't need.

We don't need many of the things that we say we need in order to be happy. We have built a false identity around external things and have forgotten that we have a vast internal world that has immense power. We live and accept mediocrity for ourselves when we should be upholding high standards of self love and respect for all life. It is also for old systems that no longer serve the greater good to collapse so that a new paradigm can be born. It's a good thing, ultimately.

We can consider this collapse a cleansing of the unnecessary so we will begin relating to life at a deeper level. At the same time, there's nothing wrong with financial abundance but it needs to be married with our hearts and with genuine abundance and giving for all. We all need to be contributors of abundance by getting out of survival consciousness and into the realization that there's plenty for all.

Question
Four

Ahonu: Can Source comment on Trump as a president, and can we have some insight into the civil unrest after his election?

AR: The world will not accept another dictator. Trump will not last the 4-year term if he pursues a racist, dictatorial approach. He simply won't last.

In terms of the civil unrest, I see a blanket of darkness, but I see light behind it. It is like looking at a dark sky, but we know there is always brightness behind the clouds. People are causing their own ugliness right now, and it will collapse inwards on itself.

This will happen because the darkness will be vaporized by the light, but in that vaporization many people may destroy themselves. I have a lot of hope for the positive energy that is coming through, and believe it or not, some of this chaos is a form of weeding out of negativity.

People who are orchestrating violence and

destruction will cause their own demise. Source says there is a new world coming, and it may seem to take a long time, but that is what is happening. It is a ten-year period of adjustment.

Evil will not prevail over the Earth, but the collapse of it may be ugly. It is clear that those who cannot withstand these changes, and whose hearts are not pure, will not last through it. If you aren't part of what will raise the world into a brighter future, the chances are you will not survive in it.

Question Five

Ahonu: Will the current situation in Syria have a devastating effect on the world?

AR: The leadership is extending its reach and its effect in the country, but it is not a permanent situation. There is a lot more to happen in Syria as these events unfold. There will be more unrest in the short term. We are still looking at another year at least, before the outcome for Syria is decided.

I see more conflict and more countries getting involved, Russia in particular. There will be other countries involved over the next year. We will see more refugees trying to leave the country for safety. Next year is still in conflict, and I see a lot more people fleeing for their lives.

The Syrian issue could result in an escalated engagement by world powers, but it will not be on the same scale as Afghanistan, for example. It looks like Vladimir Putin doesn't have a good enough reason to be involved, but he has made himself involved so that Russia can again be seen as a world power. Russia is keen to take its place on the world stage to keep the balance of power in the region.

Question Six

Ahonu: What role does the Rothschild family play in today's world events?

AR: The Rothschild's, among others, are still very much behind the banks and the corporations. They still have their hand in the money system and the power system. We have to realize this is a tradition for these families — a way of life for them. They're not going give this up easily. The church, the banking systems, the corporations and the power elite will be the last to concede to a new paradigm. However, there have been some breaks in their chain, and the outcome is in flux right now.

Question

Seven

Ahonu: What is the best way to pray for others and the world?

AR: Our intention is really our prayer and those intentions are things that we do every day. Of course there's formal prayer which is a form of meditation and of course that is a very, very powerful way of putting positive, loving thoughts consciously and deliberately out into the world. With that type of prayer you're actually donating spiritual energy to the world. The other way is to look at where we are in our own hearts and in our own motivations and choose the high road in our choices and decisions.

We were at a conference this past weekend and the woman who was speaking was talking about her mom passing away last year. She was helping her father clean out the house and she found a journal that her mom had that she never knew she had. When she started reading it she found that her mom would deliberately write down affirmations for her children and for herself every day. She'd write these beautiful, positive statements about her children and her desires for them in their futures and she repeated them every day. By doing this, she was essentially 'praying' for her children by affirming a positive future for them.

This is a good example of what you can do for those you love and for the world. You can make a gratitude list as well and write what you're thankful for every day. You'll find there's a lot more than you think to be grateful for.

Whenever I've made a gratitude list, I find that I'm saying thanks for things that haven't yet materialized as well as those that have, knowing that they already are. These are all things you can do and they all help to transform the energy that's out there.

Question Eight

Ahonu: What are light codes?

AR: The official answer from Source is they are arrangements of geometries, music or sound that take on specific patterns to do specific things. I can use the crop circles as an example of how a pattern could be arranged in beautiful geometries that also carry particular frequencies and sound tones with them. These geometries affect the land around them and also the consciousness of the people. Light codes are similar except that they come from a much higher place. They're like blessings that get down-stepped into geometries and sounds in order to affect worlds and all the species in those worlds. Their purpose is to evolve life in some way, to activate a higher potential for all life everywhere.

* * *

Question Nine

Ahonu: How much longer will the portals remain open for the light codes coming in from Source to Earth?

AR: What I'm seeing is that we are merging into the portals — therefore I don't see the portals closing. If the portals were closing, that would mean that the Earth would be staying stationary where she is. The image I'm seeing is that the Earth is in a movement toward a merger and this merger is into more light and into time thinning. So, I don't see the portals closing.

If we all continue to do our work and keep shifting into this new consciousness, we will be moving into this new 'place' and the process will be complete.

* * *

Question Ten

Ahonu: What are some of the things we can do to make use of these light codes?

AR: On one hand, the light codes are naturally providing miracles and upgrades in consciousness and biology for people. What that means is your manifestations will occur much faster. Not only that, the light codes carry blessings, so some of the things won't have to do with your own manifestations but they will just be new opportunities where things suddenly start working out for you that haven't worked out before. So, a lot of beneficence is coming along with these light codes. The potential for healing of your body and mind and many other things is there.

How best to work with them? Begin shifting your own consciousness into what the consciousness of those light codes is — which is more Christ consciousness, more love — and an intention to bless all life everywhere.

You know, we do have to deal with our darkness. We have to deal with the parts of us that are still unhealed, still in judgment, still with limited mediocre thinking and behaviors. There are tremendous resources out there to help people move through blockages and issues. There are all sorts of holistic therapies, there's journaling about your fears and being honest with yourself about what's really going on in your life, there's accepting the truth that whatever you're experiencing is a reflection of your consciousness on some level. Body work is important now too — you'd be surprised what a great massage will do for you!

(Please note that in a following volume in this series of Answers From The Akashic Records, there is a complete book on the Light Codes.)

Question Eleven

Ahonu: When you talk about sun gazing, how long is recommended to look at the Sun? Isn't it harmful to do this?

AR: Sun gazing is very beneficial actually, because the Sun is very regenerative. The proper time to sun gaze is only when the sun rises or sets. Once the Sun comes up above the horizon, you no longer look at it. When the Sun sets, you're only looking at it right when it is going down. You're only gazing for 5 to 30 seconds.

You will find that you're feeling more centered and grounded by doing this practice. You will also have much clarity, feel stronger, and be less hungry.

Question Twelve

Ahonu: Any tips on shortsightedness?

AR: I'm getting interesting answers from Source about this. Sources is saying to sun gaze regularly for just 5 to 30 seconds when the sun is coming up/crowning and also right when the sun is setting. As time goes on, you can stretch the gaze a little longer, but be careful. Doing that will stimulate a different memory for you about your birth.

It's funny that Source said, *"when the Sun is crowning"*, because the implication is that shortsightedness could be a result of something that occurred during your birth. Any conclusion that you may have come to during your birth could be affecting your eyesight. In your case, I would consider having some rebirthing sessions that focus on your birth experience, or possibly even your conception, because it looks to me that there needs to be a new program in the brain about life itself.

Question Thirteen

Ahonu: When a person constantly sends negative thoughts, energy and intentions toward you and you feel it physically in your body, what do you do, especially when cutting chords, prayers and other methods of removal don't work? What else can we do to keep our spirits, thoughts and hearts calm in the midst of chaos?

AR: The answer Source is giving me is to remember that the whole idea of seeing another person as a separate self is the first mistake that we all make. The second part is you could go journal about what the whole experience means to you.

Treat your 3-D consciousness like a dreamscape much like you would your sleeping state. My own method of finding out what a dream means to me is to make myself everybody in the dream. You could do that exercise with the person who is bothering you.

You could make yourself them and begin to describe them as if they represented some aspect of you.

Write down in your journal, "I am (other person's name), I am (adjectives, description), etc. You go on to describe them and be as honest as you can be. Let all the adjectives and descriptions, both good and bad come out. *"I am blank blank blank"* ... and just write what comes up because there has to be a commonality between yourself and what you're experiencing with the other person.

Once you find it, oftentimes the energy will lose its power and then you are conscious and can decide differently about whatever shows up. Try that and see what happens rather than try to seal yourself off from the negative experience.

Question Fourteen

Ahonu: What does Source say for those of us who seem to be using a higher percentage of our brains? Is this really happening or is it strictly spiritual?

AR: I don't see a separation there. Source is saying brain activations can happen from many causes. A person could change their diet, for example and by doing so they could clear out portions of their brain or perhaps activate different parts of their brain just by eating better (which I find very interesting!). Our ability to avail of higher consciousness and use other parts of our brain does, to some extent, seem to be diet related. It also has to do with our own particular genetic makeup and what we have going on naturally.

Spiritually more and more people are having their brains activated just from what's happening with the Sun and with the changes in the electromagnetic field.

The light codes we just spoke of are activating our brains also. So there are many different factors going on contributing to this process. You can see evidence of this by the increase in mental telepathy, desires for more love, peace and harmony, genius potentials in science and inventions, more powerful healing abilities and modalities, etc.

Some people are born with more of their brain 'turned on' and most of these new children are like that. Meditation will also activate higher portions of the brain as will the release of negative thoughts, beliefs and judgments.

Question Fifteen

Ahonu: In olden times people would be horribly tortured for prolonged periods of time before they died. Did the spirit of the person being tortured really suffer the whole extent of this or did their spirit leave their body before it got too extreme?

AR: Remember that the spirit is the observer, the experiencer and the decider. It does receive the impact of the torture and the reason it does is that it is still in the body until it leaves it completely. Until the spirit leaves the body entirely (dies) the imprint of the experience still registers. As the spirit leaves, the imprint will still register in the cells of the body, until they die and decay. This is because all life is conscious. It is possible for the spirit to move some of itself out of the body during extreme pain, but the experience is still being registered on various levels until the spirit leaves completely.

The spirit does not withdraw itself right away; therefore it experiences torture to the extent that it is still present in the body.

In my first book 'A Time of Change,' Source explained the difference between spirit, soul and individuated spirit so that we could understand the difference between them. Source created a particular pattern for life and a particular potential and that potential is eternal and ever expanding life that goes on forever.

This pattern, or template for life, is based on love, allowance and freedom. It is what all spirit is composed of. It has all it needs for unlimited possibilities and for the actualization of those possibilities. At all times your consciousness is free. Your spirit self imprint, as you were created from Source, is a free spirit and has incredible potential but not every spirit is born at the same level of self-awareness, or consciousness.

Consider the spirits coming off Source to be like snowflakes — each snowflake is unique and different in their own way, even though they all come from water. Water is the foundational pattern from which snowflakes have their existence.

Similarly, each spirit is unique and on its own path of self-discovery once it comes off of Source, even though all spirits have the same foundational template and potential. Once a spirit becomes individualized, it is on a journey to self realization and it begins to have experiences.

When it goes through experiences it comes to

its own conclusions about those experiences and it makes associations about life and what it is thinking and believing about it. Thus, the spirit begins to create a concept of itself which it now believes is its identity. It forgets it is a spirit with unlimited power and potential and it may completely forget it is on a journey towards greater self, or God realization. It will think that the concepts and beliefs about reality it is making from its experiences, *is* itself.

If the spirit goes through a torture or trauma experience in one of its incarnations into a body, it will conclude certain things about that experience; therefore a part of the spirit is now traumatized and will need to be healed at some point.

When I do psychic surgery on someone and I look into a person's energy field, I very often see imprints of past lives where they were tortured or went through some other traumatic experience. The imprint is still there and it is still something they have to clear and forgive.

The soul is different from the spirit in that it is built up by accumulating victories and overcoming challenges in incarnations. You could also say that the soul is the mastery of the various color rays in any given dimension.

Question

Sixteen

Ahonu: Do you see free energy replacing fossil fuels in the near future?

AR: There are more and more free energy devices being made and used by small groups of individuals, so there is an uprising in it which is very positive. Two years ago I would not have been able to say that. Two years ago corporations would still have done a lot to suppress free energy but now there's a huge movement towards it.

More people are working with it and you will see it in things like automobiles or electricity. You will see progress over the next five years but it may not be completely implemented in that time frame. Perhaps in the next 10 to 20 years, depending on the growth of consciousness.

Question

Seventeen

Ahonu: Does cremation versus burial make a difference in how fast the spirit leaves the body? Should cremation be done immediately after passing or should one wait a number of days to cremate a body to allow for the spirit to completely leave?

AR: It is actually better to cremate a body because fire energy is very purifying and will cleanse the body of multiple energies that could have been attached or interwoven into the body. When you put a body in the ground that dissolution or purifying process takes a long time and sometimes astral aspects of the person linger on in the form of ghosts. Cremation on the other hand, burns off more lower energies right away. It is not necessary to wait.

Question
Eighteen

Ahonu: I heard it will take 144,000 people of higher consciousness to move the planet to a more positive higher frequency place. Is this true?

AR: 144,000 isn't nearly enough to shift the entire planet. I'm seeing we need at least 70% of the people to cause the shift you are speaking of. The reason it is 70% rather than 51% in the 100th monkey examples, is because this is still a free will planet and you really need the majority to shift over to higher consciousness by choice.

This will carry the planet forward in terms of the actualization of higher consciousness. The majority of the population needs to consciously choose a new world and become the actualization of the concept in order for the planet to be the new Earth.

Question Nineteen

Ahonu: What business concept could be started without a lot of money in a place like Germany where one could live as well as help inspire people in a huge way?

AR: The foundations that Source is suggesting to us are a cooperative and sharing business; one where everyone who participates has an equal share. It's not based on a pyramid structure — rather it's based on a sphere. What that really means is, it has to do with the collective where everyone contributes and participates and receives. There's not one person holding the brunt of the financing or control.

Instead, it's more of a team effort in terms of rebuilding a community that is based on natural laws of nourishment and responsibility to all. It is the idea of the group in relationship with and to each other.

This doesn't mean everyone is the same. Instead, a person's unique and particular gifts are utilized and acknowledged without competition. The focus is on cooperative teamwork where everyone contributes a particular asset that they have. Each person's uniqueness is validated and all contribute. The delegation of roles would be wide and varied and dependent on skills and not on competition.

The Profundities

Summary

- Our intention is our prayer.
- Prayer donates spiritual energy to the world.
- Treat your 3-D consciousness like a dreamscape much like your sleeping state.
- Light codes are naturally providing miracles in our consciousness and biology.
- Begin shifting your consciousness with an intention to bless all life everywhere.
- Sometimes a more advanced being will agree to carry a fallen being within its own biology as a way to help the fallen being rehabilitate itself.
- A cloned being does not carry the same spirit energy as the original being.
- Many governments are fed up with the insanity that has been going on with our food and our environment.
- Economic downturn is not a punishment by Source — rather it's an attempt at human balance and the return to our inward self.
- Control loses power when you find commonality between you and another person.
- We all need to be contributors of abundance by getting out of survival consciousness and into the realization

that there's plenty for all.

- Economic collapse can be a cleansing of the unnecessary.

- We have built a false identity around external things and have forgotten that we have a vast internal world that has immense power.

- Future business will have collective participants with equal shares. They will not be based on a pyramid structure — rather they will be based on a sphere.

- Light codes are blessings that get down-stepped into geometries and sounds in order to affect worlds.

- Sun gazing, when done properly, is very regenerative and grounding.

- Sun gazing can help with shortsightedness.

- More people are having their brains activated just from what's happening with the Sun.

- Meditation also activates higher portions of the brain as does the release of negative thoughts, beliefs and judgments.

- Remember that the spirit is the observer, the experiencer and the decider.

- It is better to cremate a dead body rather than bury it because fire energy is purifying.

- It will take 70% of the people to actualize a new Earth.

* * *

To get one of the thousands of profound statements from the Akashic Records in your mailbox every second day, simply register on the World of Empowerment website here: https://worldofempowerment.com.

Acknowledgements

So many of you have opened your hearts and minds to Truth, willing to be participants and creators of a new world — a world based on love, cooperation, harmony and peace. And we've had the good fortune to meet, counsel and interview many of you, all dedicated to the empowerment and awakening of mankind. We witnessed your most intimate thoughts and feelings, your fears and strengths, your human-ness!

So, it is for you we have written this series of books, *Answers From The Akashic Records*. You're willingness and thirst for truth has fueled a growth of awareness, allowing for an acceleration in the down-stepping of wisdom and knowledge. Without you, these pages would not have been published, and we would not have had the pleasure of sharing our experiences of Source!

Blessings!

Aingeal Rose & Ahonu

Aingeal Rose O'Grady & Ahonu
Transformational Catalysts and Spiritual
Visionaries

Aingeal Rose (USA) & Ahonu (Ireland) are authors, artists, speakers, researchers, ministers, radio hosts and spiritual teachers who, individually and as a Twin-Flame husband-and-wife team, have helped countless people all over the world move from mediocrity to joy, clarity and awareness through their simple but highly effective series of books, programs, workshops and online sessions.

Transformational catalysts and spiritual visionaries, Ahonu & Aingeal Rose, have witnessed their clients breaking free of emotional bondage and observed the light of awareness radiating through their eyes over and over again. This twin flame couple draws on 60 years of combined experience and expertise in self-mastery and ascension mechanics to make a profound difference in people's lives. They are trusted by clients around the world for their authentic down-to-earth approach, and are known for empowering their clients and helping to raise the consciousness of the world.

International workshops including Mastering Your Destiny, Psychic Laser Therapy, and Akashic Records Training are just a few of the courses they offer. Ahonu & Aingeal Rose are also popular media guests and co-hosts of a weekly broadcast on World of Empowerment Radio. In addition to being gifted spiritual teachers, authors, speakers, and publishers, Ahonu & Aingeal Rose are ordained ministers in the non-denominational Alliance of Divine Love Ministry, bringing that devotion into everything they do.

Ahonu & Aingeal Rose are often referred to as "freedom facilitators", effectively combining spiritual guidance and intuition with eye-opening readings of the Akashic Records. These sessions bring clients into alignment with their soul's purpose and free them from old beliefs that have held them hostage throughout their lifetimes. The Akashic Records are a database direct from Source that answers life-changing questions from each individual's own record of their many lifetimes and sojourns in Spirit.

Along with being the authors of this 100-book series of Answers From The Akashic Records, Aingeal Rose is the author of two other books, "A Time of Change" and "The Nature of Reality." These books share the wisdom from the Akashic Records on a variety of topics that allows readers to discover life-changing insights. Ahonu is the author of "The Reincarnation of Columbus", which is an honest and gripping autobiography telling his true-life story of how a man copes with grief and loss and transforms it into personal empowerment and joy.

Having the unique distinction of being twin flames, Ahonu & Aingeal Rose, share a unique bond that enhances their ability to help others. For example, they offer a memorable and joyful wedding ceremony for couples desiring a celebration that strengthens the Divine masculine and feminine bonds between them. Together they founded Holistic Ireland, the World of Empowerment Organization the Spirit of Love Project and the 8-Steps-to-Freedom program.

They work throughout the United States and Ireland, are Master Tarot Teachers, an authority on the Akashic Records and hold certifications in Psychic Laser Therapy, Kathara Healing, Soul Retrieval, Reiki and Cellular Re-Patterning. They have held workshops in Manifesting, Self-Healing, Working with Homeopathic Color Remedies, Beginner through Advanced Tarot, Visionary Art and more.

On the http://worldofempowerment.com website you will find testimonials, podcasts, healing services, home study courses, private consultations, books, audio books, mp3 downloads and more. Audio programs are easily downloadable on your iPad, iPod, or iPhone.

For further information or to arrange an interview, book signing, speaking engagement, book a workshop, Spirit of Love painting or

Akashic Records consultation, contact them on http://worldofempowerment.com or by Phone USA: +1-224-588-8026 or Skype: ah-hon-u

ahonu@ahonu.com

aingealrose@aingealrose.com

Disclaimer

Address all inquiries to:
Twin Flame Productions LLC,
1462 SW 27th St., Redmond, OR 97756
http://twinflameproductions.us

Connect With Aingeal Rose & Ahonu

BLOG: worldofempowerment.com/wp/
YOUTUBE: youtube.com/user/
ahonuandaingealrose
TWITTER: twitter.com/ahonu
PINTREST: pinterest.com/aingealrose/
FACEBOOK: facebook.com/
newworldofempowerment
LINKEDIN: linkedin.com/in/
kevinogrady

Spirit of Love Project: ahonu.com/
spiritoflove
Spirit Gallery: ahonu.com/gallery/
index.php/spiritoflove
Aingeal Rose's website:
aingealrose.com
Ahonu's Website: ahonu.com
Holistic Ireland: holistic.ie
Sacred Sites Tour of Ireland:
mysticalireland.holistic.ie
Sacred Earth Waters:

SacredEarthWaters.com
World of Empowerment:
WorldofEmpowerment.com

**Ahonu.com, AingealRose.com,
WorldofEmpowerment.com**

More to Explore

Thanks for reading! If you enjoyed this book or found it useful, we'd be grateful if you'd post a short review on Amazon. Your support really makes a difference! Here are more of our works for you to explore:

AKASHIC RECORDS PODCAST
Every Saturday at 10am PST, AHONU & Aingeal Rose discuss each question and answer from this book, and in turn work their way through the entire 100-book series. Listen to the archives at http://answersfromtheakashicrecords.com or subscribe on iTunes here: http://apple.co/2iVxWwq

AINGEAL ROSE & AHONU PODCAST
Every month Twin Flames AHONU & Aingeal Rose interview exciting guests on The Honest-to-God Series on World of Empowerment Radio on the 1st Saturday of each month at 10am PST. Listen to the archives at http://honesttogodseries.com or subscribe on iTunes here: http://apple.co/2j9kaFT

AKASHIC RECORDS — Online Group Sessions
Held on the 1st Sunday of every month online, these group Akashic Record sessions allow you to bring your big questions to Source. ONLY for spiritual/universal/global inquiries of the Universe, not for personal questions. More info here https://worldofempowerment.com/wp/events

AKASHIC RECORDS TRAINING
Accelerate your spiritual knowledge by learning to read the Akashic Records. Come away with skills

enabling you to be an Akashic Records reader. Use the insight and knowledge for your own, your family or become a full practitioner. This is a small intimate training held in the USA and in Ireland — also available online at http://akashicrecords.smartmember.com.

SPIRIT ART
Explore your own Inner Self through art! YOU NEED NO ART EXPERIENCE for this class! AHONU will guide you through various fun-filled exercises that stimulate your intuitive self and inner child to come out and paint! This class is fun, spiritually revealing, and highly transformative. USA and Ireland — not available online. All Materials Provided.

TWIN FLAME / SOUL MATE LECTURE
How do you know if you have met your Twin Flame or a Soul Mate? What are the signs? What is their purpose? Are you in a Twin Flame relationship? What are the challenges and rewards? Includes a copy of our Twin Flames & Soul Mates eBook. This lecture answers these questions and more. USA, Ireland and eBook.

TRANSFORMATIONAL WRITING
This online class will free you from many unwanted belief systems and return your own power to you. By exploring your own consciousness, you will bring many beliefs to light and put yourself in the driver's seat of choice once again. This is a powerful class using a simple tool that is yours forever. Enroll here: http://tw.smartmember.com

PSYCHIC LASER THERAPY for PRACTITIONERS
Within the human auric field are layers of interwoven energies containing a history of our past lives, belief patterns, joys and sorrows and more. The condition of our chakra system and

magnetic web is also held here. These appear as living images and events in our fields, affecting who we are today. This class is a form of etheric surgery designed to remove imprints, blockages, and trauma held within these layers thus freeing your client from lifetimes of accumulative karma. The results are: increased energy, clarity, accelerated manifestation of desires, feeling light and clean and a greater sense of Self. This is a certification course and extends over 2 days — Day 1 is Text and procedure; Day 2 is practical application. This is a small intimate training held in the USA and Ireland — not available online.

THE 8 STEPS TO FREEDOM
This program was originally 8 weeks, starting on the 8 day of the 8 month at 8pm for 88 minutes — it is now online for your convenience and to take at your leisure! Meet with AHONU & Aingeal Rose online as they deliver life-transforming outcomes, make sense of your life, understand your relationships, accelerate your possibilities and help you grow in peace and wisdom. This series was developed by AHONU & Aingeal Rose to fulfill specific desires people need, help deliver specific results people want and to solve specific challenges people have. Visit: http://8-steps-to-freedom.com

Details of all workshops/courses from https://worldofempowerment.com/wp/events

AHONU & AINGEAL ROSE

Other Books by
Aingeal Rose & Ahonu

This is Aingeal Rose & Ahonu's entire book library at the time of publication, and they are publishing more books all the time. Find out every time they publishes a book, by signing up for their alerts below. <u>On Amazon (search for AHONU or AINGEAL ROSE)</u>

Answers From The Akashic Records (in 100 Volumes)
A Time of Change by Aingeal Rose
The Nature of Reality by Aingeal Rose
The Reincarnation of Columbus by Ahonu
Ayurveda, Ayur Veda, Ajurveda
Essential Info About Aromatherapy Essential Oils
Healing With Reiki
Indigo, Crystal & Rainbow Children
Quickest Way to Knowing Acupuncture & Acupressure
Spirit Art, Soul Portraits & Ancestral Healing
Twin Flames & Soul Mates

AHONU has also provided graphic design and editorial support to these authors for the following Amazon books:

Animal Guides, Protectors, Totems, & Power Animals by Chantal Cash
What is Dowsing? By Chantal Cash
Dowsing; An Art of Intention by Chantal Cash

Ensure you get Aingeal Rose & Ahonu's next book.
Sign up for book alerts here!

https://WorldOfEmpowerment.com

Made in the USA
Coppell, TX
01 June 2022

78379263R00039